It's Just Good Teaching:
Ideas to Add to Your Bag of Tricks

Grades 3rd-6th

By Dr. Floyd Cogley, Jennifer Kruk-Carcich, and Marcy Pollinger-Di Eduardo

authorHOUSE®

AuthorHouse™
1663 Liberty Drive
Bloomington, IN 47403
www.authorhouse.com
Phone: 1-800-839-8640

First published by AuthorHouse 6/28/2010

ISBN: 978-1-4520-2525-4 (sc)
ISBN: 978-1-4520-2526-1 (e)

Library of Congress Control Number: 2010907660

Printed in the United States of America
Bloomington, Indiana

This book is printed on acid-free paper.

Acknowledgements

To all former Graduate Students of Creative Cornerstones and Franciscan University of Steubenville that have made and continue to make the conference a safe place to learn and share,
IT'S JUST GOOD TEACHING

To Merrilee Currie, M.A., past Cornerstone participant, Special Education teacher, and daughter of Dr. Cogley, who took time from her busy personal and professional life to edit our book.

To Jennifer Zausmer-Terry, graphic designer, who donated her time and expertise to design our fabulous front and back covers.
She can be reached at zausmer18@hotmail.com

To Christopher Carcich and Peter Di Eduardo, the great husbands and Daddies, who lovingly took care of the four little boys and new little girl while their Mommies stayed up late working on this book.

To a very special lady who excused her husband from 35 years of family celebrations in June so he could be on site at all his summer conference sessions. Thank you, Barb, for your continued support of my many educational endeavors.

Without the unselfish consent given by the following Creative Cornerstones participants this book of outstanding teaching strategies would never have been assembled.

Susan Albrecht

Pat Allegrucci

Nancy Bain

Joyce Bond

Kathryn Jewell-Quigley

Jennifer Kruk-Carcich

Nancy McCune

Debbie Miller

Linda Milless

Bonnie Mills

Margaret E. Mosure

Donna Niro

Deborah Nordhaus

Rodrick G. Nurse

Christine Owen

Maribeth Perry

Laura Petrane

Marcy Pollinger-Di Eduardo

Carol Pullins

Kathleen Robinson

Ann Marie Schiska

Trisha Schock

Kathy Slotwinski

Table of Contents

It's Just Good Teaching!!!

Welcome to It's Just Good Teaching! We hope you can tell by the title that this book is designed for you, by teachers who believe in a fun, exciting, and timeless approach to learning. All of the activities in this book have been inspired by a compilation of ideas submitted by various teachers from all across the U.S.A. We have taken these ideas and designed activities that are teacher-friendly as well as easily adaptable for any lesson plan format. (You know – just the way your supervisor likes it!)

The book has a few key features that will allow you to navigate through it with comfort and ease. What more could any teacher want?

For our visual learners, we have used certain symbols in the top right corner of each page to designate the curricular area(s) of the activity. Here are your symbols:

 = Language Arts

 = Math

 = Social Studies

 = Science

Following each activity you will find:

Teacher Talk

What is Teacher Talk, you ask? Well, basically it's our way of talking to you in a more informal way — as if we were in the teacher's lounge. You will get to see a bit of our personalities come out in this section. It's a down-to-earth, real life explanation of how to individualize, enrich, remediate, and/or customize the activities to meet the needs of your particular students. Our suggestions have been applied in our classrooms and they helped to make each activity a huge success.

We hope that you enjoy reading through and using the book as much as we have enjoyed writing it. Remember, no matter where you work, who you teach, or what programs you use: In order to be a happy and successful teacher, at the end of the day, you should be able to say, "It's Just Good Teaching!"

A Day at the Museum

Objectives: SWBAT retell a story using real objects
SWBAT provide a written description of objects and how they relate to text

Grade Level: 3 - 6

Materials:
- Guided Reading/Literature Circle books
- Large index cards
- Objects from home, pictures from any media source
- Audio recording device (optional)
- Response sheet

Directions:
This activity is designed for your Guided Reading or Literature Circle groups as a culminating activity which checks for comprehension. As the students are working through their books, explain to them that their final project will be to create a museum display that will represent the highlights of their books. Students should be taking notes while reading the story to keep track of any important events that may be vital for their museum. Be sure that during the Guided Reading/Literature Circle time, there are periodic opportunities for the students to discuss their views on what they would want to put in the museum and why. Once their books are completed, each student in the group will be responsible for bringing in one item/picture of an item which best represents that part of the story. Along with the item, each student will be responsible for a written description on the index card connecting the object to the story. (Length of writing to be determined by the teacher.) Once all objects are in, the group will need to get together again to write introduction (including title) and conclusion cards, sequence objects, peer edit written descriptions for completeness and accuracy, and set up display. The display should have description cards in front of each object.

Once all museum displays are set up, students will be selected to visit the museum. Ideally, this would occur during your D.E.A.R./S.S.R./Independent Reading times or during your next reading class. After students have visited the entire museum, they will write a response about which book they would most like to read next and why.

Teacher Talk...

If you really want to jazz things up and make it seem like a very authentic museum, you can have each group record their written descriptions onto an audio recording device. As the students visit each display, rather than just reading the cards, they can listen to the students of each group share their ideas. Knowing that they will be recorded and others will be listening may encourage your reluctant writers to write just a little bit more or in a more expressive way. This is a wonderful display to leave up for parents during a time when they may be coming to school. Put them in the hallway for conferences!

Name: _____ Date: _____

Take your time and visit each book's museum display. After you have enjoyed all of the highlights from each book, take a moment to think about which book you would like to read next.

The book I would like to read:

_____

I would like to read this book because:

_____
_____
_____

Which item(s) in that book's display inspired you the most and why?

_____
_____

Celebrate Book Characters, C'mon!

Objectives: SWBAT identify the attributes/actions of a story character
SWBAT describe a connection between a tangible object and a story character
SWBAT utilize writing skills

Grade Level: 3 - 6

Materials:
- Reading material (either Shared, Guided, or Independent Reading)
- A student-selected object
- Construction paper
- Activity sheet/rubric

Directions:

After completing a book, this activity can be used as an assessment piece to have the students delve into the attributes/actions of their favorite character. You will explain that their project will be to design a birthday card for their chosen person. Show them the rubric of what the expectations will be for the process and final product. After making their selections, the students will design a web stating major events directly linked to their person. (Matt threw a ball into his neighbor's window.) The web may also include adjectives that describe the character. (Non-athletic) Once the web is complete, the students will generate a list of possible gift ideas for the character. They can highlight a final gift choice as well as the supporting details from the web.

Utilizing the information from their webs, the students will create a birthday card for their character. The contents should include, but not be limited to: the character's name, the book's title, the rationale behind the present, and the student's signature. Based on the writing skills of your students, this can be done in paragraph or essay format.

Once birthday cards are finished, the students will come in the next day with their wrapped gifts in hand. Please encourage students not to go out and buy something new. Gifts can be student-made, something from home, or a picture representing the item. Depending on teacher preference on how to do so, the students will share their gifts and cards with their peers. While observing presentations, the teacher will collect birthday cards and rubrics for scoring.

Teacher Talk...

Depending on your time and energy, you can turn this into a big class party where the students actually come dressed as their character. You can go wild decorating your classroom for this big birthday celebration and even bring in a cake to enjoy! If you're not into the party thing, this can simply become one of your choices for book report projects.

By the way, if you haven't figured it out already, sing the title just like that good old wedding song favorite!!!

Name: _____ Date: _____

Select your favorite character from the book. Write his or her name in the center of the circle below. Create a web using the character's personality traits and major events linked to him or her. Using the information from the web, create a list of possible birthday gifts you would give that character.

○

Possible Gifts: _____ _____
_____ - _____

Celebrate Book Characters, C'mon! Rubric

	Excellent	Good	Fair	Unsatisfactory
Completed web/gift list	4	3	2	1
Gift relevance supported	4	3	2	1
Character name/title/signature	4	3	2	1
Capitalization/punctuation	4	3	2	1
Correct spelling	4	3	2	1

20=100	17=89	14=83	11=77	8=71	5=63
19=95	16=87	13=81	10=75	7=69	
18=91	15=85	12=79	9=73	6=67	

Notes:

_____
_____
_____
_____
_____

Teacher: Photocopy both activity pages back to back for each student.

Guess Who?

Objective: SWBAT write a detailed five-sentence paragraph

Grade Level: 3 - 4

Materials:
- Flipbook – 6 pages per student
- Photo of each child
- Rubric (optional)

Directions:

The goal of this lesson is to foster the ability to add details when writing. The students will be given an assignment to write about themselves. Tell the students that they will be writing to give the reader clues. By the end of their finished product, the reader should be able to guess who they are reading about. Ask your students to brainstorm words that describe them, their personalities, or things that they do. Show students a sample flipbook. You can either show them one you have created about yourself or a sample from a previous year's class. After the students have completed their brainstorming, they will move on to develop their own Guess Who? flipbook. On the first page, they will write a topic sentence. Pages 2-4 will contain supporting detail sentences. Page 5 will be the closing sentence, revealing their identity. On page 6, students will compile their sentences into a fully developed paragraph, which will be written above their photos. As a culminating activity, you can put all finished flipbooks into a basket and pick one at random. One student will read it and see if he/she can identify the author.

Teacher Talk...

PERFECT BACK TO SCHOOL NIGHT BULLETIN BOARD!!! Need we say more???
Actually, yes, we do! For your photographs, a digital camera can be your very best friend. Ask your computer specialist if there is one you can use if your grade level does not already share one.

Flipbook Directions: Use 3 pieces of paper to make your 6-page book. Place page 1 down. Place page 2 on top of page 1 leaving the bottom one inch of page one exposed. Place page 3 on top of page 2, leaving the bottom one inch of page 2 exposed. At this point you will have 3 staggered pages. Pick up the stack and begin to fold the top portion of pages backwards. You will begin to see that your original 3 steps meet the bottom 3 steps. Adjust your fold so that all steps are equal in size. Staple the top at the fold to bind book.

Name: _____ Date: _____

Guess Who? Paragraph Rubric

	Excellent	Good	Fair	Unsatisfactory
Clue creativity	4	3	2	1
Punctuation	4	3	2	1
Varied sentence structure	4	3	2	1
Neat handwriting	4	3	2	1
Correct spelling, capitalization	4	3	2	1

20=100	17=89	14= 83	11=77	8=71	5=63
19=95	16=87	13=81	10=75	7=69	
18=91	15=85	12=79	9=73	6=67	

Notes:

_____
_____
_____
_____
_____
_____
_____
_____
_____

Teacher: Photocopy one per student.

Acrostic Retell

Objectives: SWBAT retell events of a story
SWBAT utilize an Acrostic Poem format to retell a story

Grade Level: 3 - 6

Materials:
- Student books
- Writing paper

Directions:

After students have read a story in class or after a book from Guided Reading/Literature Circles, the students will have the opportunity to retell events from the book using an acrostic poem. On a blank piece of writing paper, the students will write the title of the book. Under or next to each letter (depending on which direction the students want their poem) the students will use each letter of the title for the beginning word of each sentence.

For shorter stories, the students can retell events from the entire story. For chapter books, the students may complete a poem for every 2-3 chapters, collecting each finished acrostic as they go. The students may also write one final culminating acrostic at the end of the book to demonstrate a complete summary of the book. For books with shorter titles, such as <u>Holes</u>, the students may be asked to write a paragraph for each letter of the title to create more of a challenge.

Teacher Talk...

If you would like to do a great lesson on acrostic poems, an excellent interactive website is readwritethink.org. This activity is also great to summarize knowledge about historical figures. The students must research the person and write a sentence for each letter of the person's name. Another challenge might be to retell a story using every letter of the alphabet.

Spelling Circle

Objectives: SWBAT review spelling orally

SWBAT actively participate and practice listening skills

Grade Level: 3 - 6

Materials:
- Spelling word list
- Activity sheet

Directions:

In this activity, the students will be reviewing and reinforcing weekly spelling words in a small group setting. While meeting in a small group, the students will sit in a circle. You will need to have the weekly spelling list available for your eyes only. Each student will have an activity sheet and a pencil. Choose a starting person and call out the first word. The starting student repeats the word and says the first letter. The next student says the following letter of the word and so on until the word is complete. If one of the students does not know the next letter or is incorrect, the group continues until the word is complete and correct. The student who did not know his/her letter will add that word, correctly spelled, to his/her word list. That word list will be used as a study guide to be practiced at home for the upcoming spelling assessment. Continue in this fashion until all words are complete. Make sure that any student who does not know the next letter or is incorrect places that word on his or her word list. For each new word, you will start where you left off in the circle.

Teacher Talk...

Adding this activity to your spelling reviews will spice up what could be a pretty mundane task. Even your most reluctant speller will have to be on his or her toes for this one. This is a great way for the students narrow down what they truly need to study and will help with their own time management. It's a great activity to teach the parents as well. This could be great fun – and very educational – at the dinner table!

Name: _____ Date: _____

<u>Spelling Words To Study</u>

_____

_____

_____

_____

_____

_____

_____

_____

_____

_____

Teacher: Copy one or more per student as need be.

Chain Reaction

Objective: SWBAT sequence events in fiction and non-fiction texts

Grade Level: 3-6

Materials:
- Strips of multi-colored paper
- Stapler
- Student texts (optional)
- Rubric
-

Directions:

This activity can be used in conjunction with your Literature Circles or with your Science or Social Studies texts. After reading a given portion or chapter of text, the students will be placed into groups of at least 5 students. Each student will be provided a strip of paper (link). Each student will write his/her name on one side of the link.

By this age, the students are very familiar with story-mapping to demonstrate comprehension and recall. In this lesson, story-mapping skills will be utilized in both an individual and group format. Each group of students will form a line. The teacher will then instruct the group to retell the story by having each student write one event. The challenge will be that each member must tell an event based on his/her order in line. The teacher will pass out a rubric to each group or post a large-size rubric for the whole class to view. This will help the students to understand the expectations. Once the rubric is reviewed, the students will begin writing. Students will not be allowed to converse with one another or view one another's links during this process. This requires students to evaluate not only their placement in line, but also how that correlates to the sequence of events in the story. For example, a student in the middle should not record an event at the end of what was read.

Once the writing portion is complete, the students will line up their links based on their placement in line. As a group, the students will assess their finished product. If the events are truly in order and all parts of text/chapter are represented, the students will use a stapler to assemble the chain link. Upon assessing, if the students detect that an event is out of order or incorrect, they will have a chance to make corrections. We suggest that younger grades receive an opportunity to correct/rearrange 2 links. Upper grades may only receive one opportunity to make a change. Upon agreement of the final product, each group will hand in a completed chain along with incorrect links. The teacher will assess each chain against the requirements on the rubric. Completed rubrics will be handed back to the students for their own evaluation of their efforts.

Teacher Talk...

While this activity provides a wonderful challenge for small groups, there are endless possibilities to enhance whole group instruction. If the students have all been working on the same story, place the students in chapter groups. (Group 1 – chapter 1-3...) At the end of the activity, put all chain links together for a complete retell of the story. For Social Studies, assign groups into battles. The students can sequence events of that battle. At the end, put all chain links together for a full recall of the entire war. Don't forget about Science!!! What a great way to assess knowledge of the process of the Digestive System! Oh, the fun you can have! Who needs store-bought posters and bulletin boards? The chain links can be a terrific way of decorating your classroom throughout the whole year.

Name: _____ Date: _____

Chain Reaction Rubric

	Excellent	Good	Fair	Unsatisfactory
Retold major events	4	3	2	1
Sequence of events	4	3	2	1
Link from each group member	4	3	2	1
Corrections made/none needed	4	3	2	1
Correct spelling, capitalization	4	3	2	1

20=100	17=89	14= 83	11=77	8=71	5=63
19=95	16=87	13=81	10=75	7=69	
18=91	15=85	12=79	9=73	6=67	

Notes:

_____

_____

_____

_____

_____

_____

_____

_____

Teacher: Photocopy one per student.

Surveying the Scene

Objectives: SWBAT gather information from a large group of people
SWBAT analyze data
SWBAT represent data in a visual format
SWBAT utilize interviewing techniques

Grade Level: 3-6

Materials:
- Teacher-created survey
- Grid paper
- Poster board
- Student-selected project material

Directions:
A survey is a wonderful way to learn about other people and to teach students how to apply math skills to real world information. Prior to beginning this lesson, review appropriate interviewing techniques. Lead your class in a discussion about surveys and reasons for data collection. (Customer service, marketing strategies, product satisfaction, etc.) If possible, show your students an actual survey from a company or product.

You will then provide each student with a copy of the teacher-created survey. Allow students to begin collecting data among the class. You will need to float around and facilitate to keep the momentum going and to make sure students are on task. Once the data is collected, ask the students how a visual representation of the data could be created. This is the point where you need to tailor this to your own math program. If you are learning about bar graphs, lead your discussion that way. If you are learning about pie graphs, lead the discussion that way.

Either the next day in class or for homework, the students will take the data they have collected and represent it in a visual format. If all goes well, the graphs should look amazingly similar as the data they have collected is exactly the same. Allow the students to present their information in small groups.

Collect papers for evaluation. This lesson can be repeated as different graphing skills are covered throughout the year. As the students progress in their survey skills, you may have them go beyond the classroom walls as an end of the year project. They can then select their own survey topic and method for data analysis.

Teacher Talk...

Percent circles anyone?? What a great way to apply this skill in the real world. This lesson can even be used to find the mean, median, mode and range of answers.

Name_____Date_____

Directions: Use this survey to collect data from every student in your class.

1. Do you own a pair of sneakers?   Yes_____ NO_____

2. Do you play a team sport?   YES_____ NO_____

3. Do you play an individual sport? YES_____ NO_____

4. Do you like outdoor activities?   YES_____ NO_____

5. Do you watch sports?   YES_____ NO_____

6. Do you exercise?   YES_____ NO_____

7. Do you consider yourself athletic? YES_____ NO_____

_____

Teacher: Photocopy one per student.

Shopping for Word Problems

Objectives: SWBAT solve word problems

SWBAT develop word problems

Grade Level: 3 - 6

Materials:

- Newspaper grocery ads
- Calculators (optional)
- Scratch paper
- Student recording sheets

Directions:

Using the grocery ads from the weekly newspaper, the students will make up word problems using prices/foods. Each student will be responsible for completing two recording sheets. On the first sheet, the student will create and write 3 separate word problems. On the second sheet, he/she will write the word problems again, this time showing the solution processes and answers. The students will give the completed second sheet to the teacher. The first sheet will be stapled to the appropriate advertisement page so that students can use it while solving the problems. These word problem packets can be placed in a math center or exchanged by students in pairs. The teacher will collect the completed packets to be graded. What a great way to get 2 assessments done at once by having the students generate and solve original word problems.

Teacher Talk...

The younger students may be working on multiplication while the upper grades may be working on budgeting skills.

Here is one example of a simple word problem just to help you get started...

"How much will 3 lbs. of grapes cost if one pound costs $2.90?"

You can certainly do this on a weekly basis. The students can bring in their own advertisements or you can keep a collection of your own in the classroom to be used at anytime.

As Easy As Pie

Objectives: SWBAT create and read a pie graph

SWBAT identify fractional parts

SWBAT convert fractions into percentages

SWBAT identify mean, median, mode and range of a set

Grade Level: 3-6

Materials:

- One 1.64 ounce bag of candy-coated chocolate bits for each student
- One 8 ½ "x 11" piece of paper for each student
- Crayons to match colors of the candy
- Ruler
- Pencils
- Recording sheet

Directions:

The students will sort the colors of a 1.64-ounce bag of candy-coated chocolate bits (or other small candies). They will group the candy bits by color and record the amounts of each color on recording sheet. The students will also record the total amount of candy in their bags as well as compute the mean, median, mode, and range. Next, they will create the circumference of a circle on the 8 ½ x 11 piece of paper with the candy bits. (Make sure they are touching and lined up according to color.) Once the circle is made, the students will trace on the inner part of the ring of candy to draw a circle. They should then find the center point and draw a dot in the middle of the circle. (If your students have already been introduced to a compass, now would be a great time to utilize it.) The students will use the ruler to draw lines, forming pie pieces from the edge of each color to the center of the circle. They can then color in each pie piece according to the color of the candy. Before removing the candy, students should label each slice of pie with the number of candy bits in that slice, each fractional part of the pie, and/or the percentage of the whole pie each slice represents, depending on your students' abilities. When the pie is completed, they can eat the candy.

Teacher Talk...

As with all great math lessons, the use of math vocabulary ("math talk") can extend the challenge opportunities of this activity. This lesson can work very well as an individual activity. To make it more cooperative, it might be fun to work in small groups where the students in each group collaborate to find the mean, median, mode, and range for their totals of candy (as found on their recording sheets). If you want them to have more practice for mean, median, mode, and range, you can have your students do so for each individual color.

* Just a reminder... Food allergies are always a concern. Please check with your class first and read food labels to ensure that the candies that you choose are safe for your entire class to eat. Some candy-coated chocolates are made in factories that process peanuts. Fruit ring cereal is a good alternative.

Name: _____ Date: _____

Amount of Candy	Fractional Part	Percentage
Brown _____	Brown _____	Brown _____
Red _____	Red _____	Red _____
Green _____	Green _____	Green _____
Orange _____	Orange _____	Orange _____
Yellow _____	Yellow _____	Yellow _____
Blue _____	Blue _____	Blue _____
Total _____	Total _____	Total _____

Mean	Median	Mode	Range

My group's totals are: _____ _____ _____ _____ _____ _____

Mean	Median	Mode	Range

Teacher: Copy and use sections as applicable to your students.

Action-Packed Averages

Objectives: SWBAT collect data

SWBAT calculate averages

Grade Level: 3 - 4

Materials:
- Recording sheet
- Basketball
- Jump rope
- Tape measure
- Bubbles
- Stop watches

Directions:

After you have completed your preliminary study of averages, this is a great kinesthetic way of reviewing and reinforcing this skill. You will create center areas on your playground/blacktop or in your gymnasium for the students to participate in various physical tasks. The tasks may include, but not be limited to: the number of foul shots made in a minute, successful jumps while jumping rope for one minute, the number of bubbles blown via a bubble wand in one minute, the distance jumped from a standing position, and a timed 50-yard dash. Explain to your students that each member of their group will complete each activity. The students will collect each person's data on the recording sheets as they complete their activity centers. The data will be used to calculate the average number of shots made for each group, the average number of bubbles blown, etc...

Divide your students into small groups. Assign each student a buddy within his/her group. The buddies will be responsible for counting/measuring their partner's scores, recording those scores, and sharing the results with their group. Assign each group a starting center. Using a timer, each group will spend 5-8 minutes at each center to allow for the whole group to complete it. Once the timer goes off, the groups will rotate clockwise to the next center. Repeat until each group has completed each center. Allow time for each group to sit and meet briefly to go over results to make sure the scores/measurements are accurate and complete. Finally, the students will calculate their group's averages for each center.

Teacher Talk...

    A great way to close this activity is to have the students present their information. You can simply have a spokesperson from each group share the results as you mark the information on your chalk/white board. You can also use all of this information to calculate the averages among your whole class. This, of course, does not need to be done on the same day, as your kids may be tired from all that exercise!!! What a great excuse to dress down for the day.

Name: _____ **Date:** _____

Record your data below. Once you have completed all activities be sure to double-check your data among your group. Then calculate your group's averages.

Foul shots made in 1 minute
___ ___ ___ ___ ___ ___
Average # of shots made:

Jumps made in 1 minute
___ ___ ___ ___ ___ ___
Average # of jumps made:

Bubbles blown in 1 minute
___ ___ ___ ___ ___ ___
Average # of bubbles blown:

Distance jumped
___ ___ ___ ___ ___ ___
Average distance jumped:

Time to complete a 50 yard dash
___ ___ ___ ___ ___ ___
Average # of time:

Teacher: Photocopy one per student.

The Non-Worksheet Worksheet

Objective: SWBAT reinforce any math skills

Grade Level: 3 - 6

Materials:
- Chalkboard/whiteboard, chart paper
- Non-worksheet worksheet (attached)

Directions:

Your "Do Nows" will never be the same! At the beginning of the month, the teacher will write a particular math problem on the whiteboard/chalkboard/chart paper for the students to copy in the first square of their non-worksheet worksheet. The students then solve the given problem. They will store the worksheet in their binders/folders. This process is repeated everyday for the month with a new problem each day being copied and solved. The problems should reflect the skills being taught in your class at the time. (We suggest sticking with the same skill for a week at a time.) At the end of 20 days, the teacher will collect the papers and score them. This not only allows the teacher to assess who has mastered the skills and who needs some remediation but also allows for a grade to be given for "Do Nows" which often go unchecked.

Teacher Talk...

Keeping with this basic format, you can assess just about any skill! What a no-brainer! One sheet for quick assessment of knowledge of the periodic table, events in history, events in a given literature chapter, parts of speech identification...the list is endless. One more thing....YOU'RE WELCOME! ☺

Name _____ Month _____

Teacher: Photocopy one per student.

Bingo Schmingo

Objectives: SWBAT review math skills

SWBAT match a numerical computation to its answer

Grade Level: 3-6

Materials:
- Paper
- Pencil
- Flashcards – either store-bought or teacher-made

Directions:

This game is a variation of BINGO. Each student makes his/her own Schmingo Board on a piece of paper. (Scrap paper is fine.) Depending on the age or skill level of the students, they will each pick 6 or more random numbers and write them on their sheet of paper.

Sample:

282	219
266	207
243	299

Our suggestion is to limit their range of numbers. For example, you may want to have them select only 3-digit numbers in the 200's or numbers from the 12 times-table.

The teacher, at a quick and constant pace, flashes math facts. As the cards are shown, the students cross off the answer if it is on their board. As they cross off the answer, they need to write down the math problem above it. The first person to cross out all of his or her numbers calls out, "SHMINGO!" and wins.

Teacher Talk...

Such a simple game can be used for review for any computation test. Obviously addition, subtraction, and multiplication work beautifully, but skills such as reducing fractions, converting fractions to decimals or even measurement conversions are just a few skills that can be used in this game. As a homework assignment, the students can make a set of flashcards and boards to be used in the classroom. This can be a great way to differentiate instruction. You can assign a given skill to each student depending on his or her needs.

How Do You Spell 94 Cents?

Objectives: SWBAT reinforce numeration skills
SWBAT generate an equation totaling a given sum
SWBAT correctly follow the order of operations

Grade Level: 3 - 6

Materials:
- Alphabet activity sheet
- Calculators (optional)
- Scratch paper

Directions:

Assign values to sequential letters of the alphabet. (a=1¢; b=2¢; c = 3¢; z = 26¢) Working individually, in pairs, or for homework, the students will have to come up with a variety of words that equal 94¢. Words, along with their corresponding equations, can be shared with the class and a class list can be generated to show how many possibilities exist. This can also challenge the students to find words that nobody else has found and to keep this list growing throughout the year.

Keeping with this basic format, the values of the letters can be changed according to the ability of the students. Integrating negative values and decimals are some options to further extend this activity. Students who have already been introduced to the order of operations can create multi-step equations showing the various operations.

Teacher Talk...

If you would like to make a poster showing the letter values, you can run the activity sheet through a poster machine. If you do not have access to one, poster board works great and it will be easy to create your own duplication of the activity sheet. Before writing the values, you may want to laminate your poster with just the title and letters. This gives you the chance to change the values throughout the year without having to make more than one poster.

As an extra challenge for your students, give them a list of words with some totaling up to 94¢ and some not. They can work through all of the equations to find out which are the 94¢ words.

Name _____ Date _____

Directions:

_____
_____
_____

A=	N=
B=	O=
C=	P=
D=	Q=
E=	R=
F=	S=
G=	T=
H=	U=
I=	V=
J=	W=
K=	X=
L=	Y=
M=	Z=

My 94¢ words:

_____

_____

_____

_____

_____

_____

Teacher: Fill in directions accordingly. Be sure to ask for work to be shown on the sheet or on scratch paper. Fill in values for each letter. Photocopy one per student.

39

Read All About It!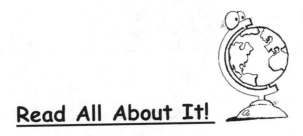

Objectives: (younger grade)
SWBAT utilize oral speaking skills SWBAT recall personal information SWBAT add details when retelling events
SWBAT discover purpose of a newspaper

Objectives: (grades 3-6)
SWBAT demonstrate note-taking skills
SWBAT gather information
SWBAT elicit details from interviewee
SWBAT write in newspaper format

Grade Level: 3-6

Materials:
- Younger Buddy class
- A newspaper
- Note-taking paper or journalism pad
- Final copy paper (should be formatted to look like a newspaper)

Directions:
After several meetings with your buddy class, pair students up for a wonderful week of sharing and writing. On Monday, the older class will gather in your meeting area. Introduce the newspaper. As you are reading the paper, plan on having your buddy class arrive. The buddy class teacher will ask you what you are doing and you will explain that you are reading through the newspaper. Invite them to join you for a group discussion on what you might learn when reading the paper. Point out how the newspaper is laid out in columns, includes pictures, and provides details about a particular event. Explain to students that they will be writing their own newspaper column based on the true stories of the younger students' week. Each afternoon, at a time that works for both classes, the partners will meet. The older student will ask the younger student to tell about that day's events. The older student will record the younger student's retelling. This will be repeated each afternoon for one week. Throughout the week, the teachers will model using various strategies and questioning techniques to elicit as many details as possible from the younger students.

The following week will be the time when the older students take the notes they have gathered and develop an individual newspaper about their buddy. Be sure to incorporate the skills that your particular grade level is working on: paragraph structure, word innovations, varied sentence structure and so on. This can be completed during the students' daily writing workshop time and/or in the computer lab.

When all students have completed their newspapers, the buddy classes will meet again to take time to "read the morning paper." The younger students will feel proud when they discover that there is a newspaper all about each one of them!

 **Teacher Talk...**

If you are not familiar with the idea of buddy classes, it is a great way to incorporate character education skills. The older students work as role models for the younger students and the younger students feel more comfortable in their school surroundings knowing there is an older friend looking out for them. Find a teacher that you enjoy working with so your creative minds can flow. When reviewing the newspaper with your classes, make sure to only show contents appropriate for that age level. You will need to go through the paper beforehand to take out anything controversial. You are not limited to a standard newspaper; you can use your PTA newspaper, school newspaper, etc.
As the older students are writing the paper, allow them to try out some of the software out there that can make this project really come to life. Ask your school's computer teacher for access to the lab so the kids can create their papers there.

Egyptian Jewelry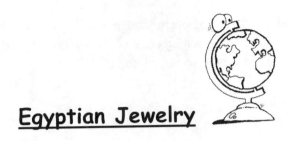

Objectives: SWBAT identify Egyptian symbols/hieroglyphics
SWBAT describe the meaning of Egyptian symbols/hieroglyphics
SWBAT create artifacts replicating Egyptian symbols/hieroglyphics

Grade Level: 4-6

Materials:
- Toaster oven
- Plasticine material (found in craft stores)
- Pin backs
- Earring hoops/ posts/backs
- Plastic jewels
- Reference material on Ancient Egypt
- Clay tools

Directions:

Egyptian history is very intriguing to most students. The people, the clothing, the buildings, and the mummies are fascinating. As a final project during your study of Ancient Egypt, allow the students to locate and replicate a piece of Egyptian jewelry that they find interesting. Students work independently to locate a picture of a piece of jewelry (bracelet, earring, necklace, arm cuff and the like) in a book or on the Internet. They are to write down whom the piece belonged to, what symbols are on it, what the symbols mean and why they are interested in this piece in particular. (Maybe a pharaoh wore the piece and it symbolized strength and a student in your class really likes the idea of being a strong- willed ruler, you get the idea.) Students should make connections on why certain symbols would have been used for certain types of Egyptians.

Once the students have their images ready and a written history of the piece approved by you, they are ready to replicate it. Using a plasticine type of material, students follow the instructions that come with it and mold the material into shape. Students should use clay tools to inscribe symbols into their jewelry and add adornments when possible. Different plastic materials require different ways to heat/mold/cool so be sure you do not place things in the oven that should not go and add the jewelry backings at the appropriate times.

Completed pieces and write-ups can be placed in a "mini museum" for a class tour or the students could wear their pieces and give a brief presentation to the class.

Teacher Talk...

With so many fashion and home design shows out here now this should be a fun and timely lesson for many of your students! Be sure to send a note home asking families if they have any costume jewelry that you could use for this lesson. You can then use parts of the pieces brought in to embellish the Egyptian jewelry.

How to Handle a Vulture

Objectives: SWBAT identify hurtful statements
SWBAT promote positive behavior
SWBAT generate coping strategies

Grade Level: 3-6

Materials:
- Toy stuffed vulture or bulletin board vulture
- Blank bulletin board space
- Basket/box
- Blank index cards

Directions:

In the beginning of the year, as you discuss classroom rules and procedures, spend a bit of time talking about what happens when people are unkind. Show your toy stuffed/bulletin board vulture. Ignite a conversation about vultures: What kind of animal is a vulture? How do they look? What do they do? How and why do they stalk weak prey? Tell students that you have even seen evidence of vultures in school each year. Ask if they think you are speaking of real vultures. Guide the discussion into how children and adults can have "vulture-like" tendencies towards others. When someone uses another's weakest point in an effort to intimidate and even hurt that person, he is truly acting as a "vulture."

In your class this year, you are going to work together to expose certain vulture statements/behaviors and practice how to appropriately handle them. Explain to your students that if they feel that someone experienced a hurtful statement or action (a vulture statement/action), they will have the opportunity to write down what was said or done and post it on the bulletin board. They will also have to write a way in which the situation was handled or could be handled better if it were to happen again. By doing this, it sends a clear message to the students in your class of what is acceptable and what is not. It also allows the students to heighten their awareness of the sensitivity of others.

It is important that the students know that writing any vulture statement is an anonymous task. The students should feel that they are safe to write how they really feel without repercussions. Model to students that you, too, post statements and actions from time to time. Sadly, it is not just students who are unkind to one another. Teachers and other adults can be unkind as well.

Make this a weekly or bi-monthly opportunity to role-play using the situations written on your bulletin board. The students can help share other possible strategies and rebuttals. After the posted vulture statements have been discussed, develop a method in which you dispose of these statements so that the affected students are freeing themselves of the hurt that has been brought to them. This also makes it clear that the class, as a whole, should not accept and allow these types of statements and actions. It should create a feeling of unity and support in the class.

Teacher Talk...

Our vision for this bulletin board is that of a lone vulture on a spooky tree. If your artistic abilities are limited, trace a vulture from a coloring book on a transparency and use your overhead projector to beam it onto bulletin board paper. Just hang the large bulletin board paper on a wall and trace the lines with marker – they come out great and your colleagues will be amazed at your new artistic prowess.

If you are not comfortable with hanging up the statements, they can simply go in a covered shoebox and can be brought out later for weekly discussions. You can let the students know that if someone writes his/her name on the statement, it is an indicator to you that the student would like to discuss that situation privately with you.

Globe Trotters

Objectives: SWBAT identify the seven continents and oceans
SWBAT label the seven continents and oceans
SWBAT correctly place the seven continents and oceans on a sphere
SWBAT divide a globe into hemispheres
SWBAT correctly place lines of longitude and latitude on a sphere

Grade Level: 3-5

Materials:
- Pumpkins – one for each child
- Permanent markers
- Paint – seven colors
- Paint brushes
- Maps and globes as references
- Rubric

Directions:

As part of your class' geography and map skills lessons, the students will be challenged to create their own globes. After a globe study, explain to the students that they will follow the criteria on the given rubric as they design their own globes. You will distribute the pumpkins and rubrics to the students. They will work independently to draw the seven continents on their pumpkins. Students will then paint and label the continents and oceans. Lines of longitude and latitude or other pertinent information could be added if desired by the teacher. We advise painting on one day and labeling the next to allow time for the paint to dry. Once students feel their pumpkin globes are complete, they will meet with a partner to discuss their work. Students will have an opportunity to share comments and suggestions with one another. After the students have met, they can go back for one last revision on their own globe. Students will hand in pumpkin globes to be evaluated.

Teacher Talk...

This lesson is great for the late fall but... if you haven't gone pumpkin picking or it's not pumpkin season, you can just as easily make paper mache spheres or look for punching balloons. (Think "old school" 1970's toy – that's the only way we know how to describe them.) If you do find the punching balloons, the students can use different color permanent markers, as paint won't adhere to balloons. Personal sized watermelons work great too

Name: _____ Date: _____

Globe Trotters Rubric

	Excellent	Good	Fair	Unsatisfactory
Located Continents & Oceans	4	3	2	1
Overall appearance	4	3	2	1
Located hemispheres	4	3	2	1
Lines of latitude/longitude	4	3	2	1
Correct spelling, capitalization	4	3	2	1

20=100   17=89   14= 83   11=77   8=71   5=63
19=95   16=87   13=81   10=75   7=69
18=91   15=85   12=79   9=73   6=67

Notes:

_____
_____
_____
_____
_____
_____
_____
_____
_____

Teacher: Photocopy one page per student.

On the Record

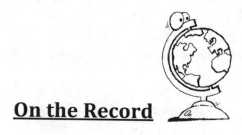

Objectives: SWBAT gather information about a historical figure
SWBAT write a report
SWBAT utilize interviewing skills

Grade Level: 5 - 6

Materials:
- Reference materials
- Writing paper
- Video tape (optional)
- Job selection straws (one short, one long)

Directions:

This is a 2-part reporting process. The second part will be a surprise for your students, so be sure not to tell them when introducing the project. The students will be asked to work with a partner to select a historical figure to investigate in order to generate a report. This can tie in with any of your social studies themes such as inventors, presidents, etc. The students will be given time to use many reference materials both in and out of school as they gather as much factual information as possible. To aid in the development of a report, the students may follow a given outline.

A possible outline to encourage and organize the research process:

Name of person

I. Childhood
- A. Birth date
- B. Place born
- C. Relevant events in childhood leading to historical importance

II. Adulthood
- A. Schooling
- B. Family and Marriage
- C. Dead (date of death) or Alive?

III. Greatest accomplishments in history
- A. Importance of accomplishments at the time they occurred
- B. Impact of accomplishments in present day society

IV. Artifacts/Clothing- This is an extra credit section where items or pictures can be added to enhance the report.

    A. Clothing that person would have worn.

    B. Items that your person would have used during their accomplishments

The students should follow your regular reporting system. Be sure they understand that they can/should bring in real items to enhance their reports on the date that you are collecting the written reports.

       The second portion of this activity occurs on the day that the written reports are due. Allow a big chunk of time for this process to be completed. The students will sit with partners and place their reports and artifacts out on their desks. The teacher will walk around and "clip board cruise" to take a peek at the artifacts. The teacher will announce that the students will be interviewing historical figures today. Tell the students that they will only be able to utilize their reports to generate the questions and answers for the interview. Student pairs will draw straws to see who will be the interviewer and who will be the historical figure. The students will have a specified amount of time (about 20 minutes) to complete their questions and answers. Interview sessions will be held in front of the class. Remind the students who are portraying the historical figures to use the props/clothing for the best presentation possible. This would be the time that you would video record the interviews. (This would make scoring the interviews easier on you as you could do them at home with a clear mind.) Depending on your schedule, you may want to do some of the interviews today and the second half the following day. Be sure to collect all reports, question cards, and materials by the end of class.

Teacher Talk...

What a great way make the students' written reports relevant. This lesson also allows for the students' diverse abilities to shine through. Even those who are not the most proficient writers can earn a great grade as they can present their information verbally and with flair!

Go, Team, Go!

Objectives: SWBAT locate states on a map

SWBAT identify state capitals

SWBAT use a map key to calculate a map distance

SWBAT graph data

Grade Level: 3 - 6

Materials:

- Large map of U.S.A.
- Local baseball team schedule
- Push pins
- Atlas/Internet (optional)
- Chart paper
- Recording sheet

Directions:

The teacher and students will discuss the duties of a statistician for a sports team. Using a computer with Internet access, the teacher will show the students how to access information and statistics for a given baseball team. For a month or more during baseball season, provide your students with a schedule of games for a local team. Create a poster size duplicate of the recording sheet as a class reference. Each student will use the individual recording sheet to record each game's data. On the chart, write the name of the statistician for each game. Prior to each game, that student will locate the state of the opposing team. Each statistician should have an opportunity to do research about that team/state prior to presenting to the class. On the map, the statistician will keep track of each state by putting a dot or pushpin on that state. The statistician will then make a brief oral presentation about the previous game's results. In addition, the statistician will share information about that day's opposing team's state. The students will record the information on their individual charts as well stating data such as distance from their home state, the state capital, or any fun and interesting facts about that state. Be sure to provide adequate resources for your students to allow greater access to facts about each state. For each new game, the statistician will report the results of the previous game. The students will record and keep a tally of wins and losses.

To integrate this into your daily math lessons, the recording sheet information can be used to teach distance conversion, probability, and graphing. For example, students can find capitals and compare distance information, decipher the most economical mode of transportation based on time and distance, and estimate the amount of gas and how much money they would need to drive there and buy tickets. The class may need access to the Internet as the tasks become more relative to real world situations.

As a culminating activity, the students may be asked to determine which game they would most like to attend if possible. Using the information gathered throughout this exercise, the students will have to support their opinions with details based on what they have learned.

Teacher Talk...

What a great way to get your sports enthusiasts fully participating in your social studies and math lessons! Tying in real world experiences and one's outside interests or hobbies is a perfect way to make learning meaningful – and fun! You, yourself, do not be a sports fan to conduct this unit. Who knows? This might be just the thing you (and your non-sporty kids) need to participate in this favorite past time. If you have a local minor league or college team, one or more of the players or one of the statisticians would probably love to come in to your class to talk with the students about baseball statistics. A field trip to a local game or practice would be a great extension of this activity.

Name: _____ Date:_____

Go, Team, Go!

Opposing Team & Date	Statistician	Score	State	Capital	Distance	State Fact

Teacher: Photocopy one or more per student

53

Turnip Planter

Objectives: SWBAT explore plant life
SWBAT identify parts of a plant
SWBAT assess the need for sunlight and water in plants
SWBAT follow the scientific process

Grade Level: 3 - 5

Materials:
- Turnips (enough for small groups or individuals to each have 3)
- Chopsticks/shish kabob skewers/very strong toothpicks (teacher's choice)
- Yarn
- Melon ball maker/ fruit spoon (something to hollow out the turnip)
- Recording sheet
- Knife (teacher only)
- Small white labels

Directions:
Give each student or group a whole turnip. Allow time to observe the plant. Activate prior knowledge about the turnip. Explain to students that they will be experimenting to see what plants need in order to grow. They will use turnips in 3 different variables: with sunlight and water, with sunlight and no water, and with water and no sunlight. They will observe and record data on a weekly basis until concrete results emerge.

To prepare the turnips, the teacher will cut them in half. The students will be using the top half of the turnips (the side with the leaves). Once the students are given the turnips, they will hypothesize what will happen to each turnip based on the amount of sunlight and water. Students will invert turnips so the cut side is up and then core and hollow out the inside of the turnips. This will create a bowl that is large enough to hold water. Next, they will insert 4 toothpicks (or other wooden stick item) around the edge of each of their three turnip bowls. The students will tie a long string of yarn to each toothpick and bring the top of the yarn together in a knot to create hanging planters. The students/groups should label each hanging planter with their names and experiment variable. The class will designate areas for each hanging turnip planter. The students will need to keep the appropriate hollow turnip bowls filled with water for the duration of the experiment. They will track the changes of their planters and document the data on their recording sheets. If all goes as planned, the planters with water and sunlight should grow vines upward around the yarn.

Teacher Talk...

   When giving the students free reign of your classroom to hang their turnip planters, you may want to have a brief discussion on appropriate places. You will find that your room looks like something out of an alien movie for a while – but that's all in the name of science!

Name _____

Hypothesis:

_____

_____

Date	Sunlight/ Water	Sunlight/No Water	Water/No Sunlight

Conclusion:

_____

_____

_____

Teacher: Photocopy one sheet per student.

The New Critter In Town

Objectives: SWBAT apply knowledge about animal adaptations
SWBAT utilize research skills

Grade Level: 3-6

Materials:
- Access to various reference materials: non-fiction animal books, encyclopedias, online search engines
- Model Magic or self-hardening clay
- Paint
- Shoeboxes (provided by students if possible)
- Craft materials
- Rubric
- Writing paper

Directions:
During a study of animals and their adaptations, the students will be invited to create their own, brand new "critter." (A critter could mean a bug or animal.) The critters will be made out of Model Magic/clay and painted appropriately. The shoeboxes will be used to create the critter's habitat. The students will then write a report about this new critter, implementing their knowledge about real animals to rationalize the critter's physical attributes and habitat surroundings. Depending on the age/expertise of your students, reports should include but not be limited to: food, exact location on the earth, lifecycle, and whether or not this critter is endangered.

This project would be a great opportunity for the students to use or be introduced to research skills. If possible, discuss the upcoming activity with your media specialist(s) so your students will also be able to access the library and/or computer lab. If it is not possible to conduct research in a library or computer lab, ask your school librarian (or town librarian) to pull literature and reference materials on animals and their habitats. Be sure to provide time for students to do independent research on this project.

As the projects are completed and returned to school, set up an area inside or outside of the classroom to create a "museum" of the students' work. Depending on the location, the reports can be placed in front of the dioramas or hung on the wall behind them. You can also opt to have the students orally present their projects. Depending on time, you can have a few students present each day throughout the week. The teacher will assess the projects via a rubric.

Teacher Talk...

This project can certainly be done as a whole class experience or as an extension option for your students. You can look at this as a challenge opportunity or a supplemental activity. If done independently, it allows the students to pace themselves accordingly and use any extra time in the classroom in a productive manner. If research is large part of your curriculum, it might be a nice idea to create a culminating celebration, inviting parents to come in to view and/or listen to projects. Setting it up as a museum would allow parents to walk freely and view each project at a more steady pace, rather than sitting and listening to 20+ reports in your classroom. The students can also decide how they want to present their project in the "museum." They could do an oral presentation and leave the report for parents to read on their own, read their own report aloud, or possibly tape record their report and have a listening station readily available at their station.

Just a little reminder... please refrain from displaying scored rubrics for others to see.

Name: _____ Date: _____

New Critter Rubric

	Excellent	Good	Fair	Unsatisfactory
Critter's habitat	4	3	2	1
Critter's appearance	4	3	2	1
Bibliography	4	3	2	1
Details in written report	4	3	2	1
Correct spelling, capitalization	4	3	2	1

20=100	17=89	14= 83	11=77	8=71	5=63
19=95	16=87	13=81	10=75	7=69	
18=91	15=85	12=79	9=73	6=67	

Notes:

_____
_____
_____
_____
_____
_____
_____
_____

Teacher: Photocopy one per student.

59

Space Food

Objectives: SWBAT collect/compare/contrast data

SWBAT identify the dehydration process and its usefulness in space travel

Grade Level: 4 -6

Materials:
- Food dehydrator
- Fresh fruits/vegetables
- Food Scales or pan balances
- rulers
- Recording sheet
- Knife (teacher only)
- Pre-dehydrated foods
- Recording sheet
- Plates

Directions:

During your unit on space, it is a great time to discuss what astronauts eat while in space. After introducing what dehydration means, allow the class to sample some dehydrated store bought foods. Discuss how the food is the same/different to foods they regularly eat. Introduce the dehydration machine and show the students the fresh fruits/vegetables you have brought in to turn into "space foods". Using the knife cut the fruits/veggies into "workable" pieces of equal sizes (depending on the size of the dehydrator you have).

Break the class into groups of two or three students and hand them a dish of designated fruit/vegetable. Each group will use the recording sheet to collect data on one piece of the fruit/vegetable in its hydrated state. They are to describe what the piece looks like, measure the size of the piece and the weight of the piece. Then the piece is placed into the dehydrator. Once all groups collect data, the dehydrator is turned on. Take one extra piece of each type of fruit/vegetable and place it on a dish and place the dish on a shelf in the room where the students can view it. The following day, allow the groups to take their pieces from the dehydrator and again record its appearance, size and weight.

Using the collected data begin a discussion on why food is dehydrated for space consumption. (Smaller size, less weight to carry into space) Ask the students to place their dehydrated pieces on another dish that you have and place that dish next to the hydrated foods dish. Tell the students that there is another reason they dehydrate the foods for space travel. Leave the two dishes out for a few days and allow the students to observe. After a few days you will see the fresh food spoiling while the dehydrated foods are still edible. Be sure to point out that dehydrated foods have a much longer shelf life than fresh foods which is imperative to space travel!

Teacher Talk...

Yummy and fascinating! We still remember tasting that dehydrated ice cream in the silver and blue wrapper when we were this age. This lesson will have the same memorable quality while sneaking in those addition, subtraction, and volume type skills. Of course you can go further and dehydrate different types of foods for fun and why not see if you can re-hydrate some of the samples?

Name _____

Hypothesis:

_____

_____

_____

Type of Food:	Looks Like	Size	Weight
Hydrated			
Dehydrated			

Conclusion:

_____

_____

Teacher: Photocopy one sheet per student.

Class Olympics

Objectives: SWBAT measure length

SWBAT compare measurements of length

SWBAT calculate mean, median, mode, and range

Grade Level: 5 - 6

Materials:
- Student record sheets
- Paper plates
- Cotton balls
- Straws
- Measuring stick and/or tape measure
- Checkers

Directions:

After introducing how to calculate mean, median, mode and range, this 2 or more day activity is perfect practice to apply these skills to real life. The teacher will briefly explain that the class will be performing indoor Olympics. There will be 4 Olympic games: Paper Plate Discus Throw, Straw Javelin, Cotton Ball Shot Put, and Checkers Curling. The teacher will have each game in a designated area of the classroom or even possibly in the hallway. The teacher will then demonstrate the proper techniques of each sport and go over any classroom management obstacles that may arise. The teacher should also demonstrate how to accurately measure each throw from the starting point to where it lands.

To begin this activity, the students will break off into pairs. The teacher will assign each pair a starting game. The students should have their recording sheets (each student should have his/her own) and writing tools with them throughout the duration of the Olympic Games. On the recording sheet provided, we suggest that each pair complete at least 5 tosses at each game. You may want to modify this to meet the needs of your schedule. Students will move from station to station, measuring and recording each attempt.

On the second or last day, the students will need to use the data they have collected from the Olympic Games to calculate the mean, median, mode, and range for each game. At this time, sheets can be collected and used as an assessment piece.

As a challenge or extension activity, throw a little science into the mix. Take the curling game as the inspiration for this. Show a video or an Internet clip of an actual curling event. Discuss with students what scientific laws make the stone move more or less quickly and why the use of brooms is a factor in the game. This is a perfect time to incorporate the unit of Newton's Laws of Motion. The teacher will present the students with the challenge of improving their curling scores by changing/improving the checkers that were previously used and/or the playing surface. The students will need time to pair up again, in or out of the classroom, to discuss/brainstorm improvements as well as time to make their new stones. The students will, of course, need time to test their new stones and to record and evaluate their new data.

Teacher Talk...

The length of your class periods will determine how many days this event will take. If you are a Science-only teacher, you may want to check in with the math teachers to correlate the timing of your units.

If are actually able to get your hands on a real curling stone, even better!

Name _____   Date _____

Directions: With your partner, complete each Olympic sport 5 times and record your measurement data. Then complete the math calculations for all the sports.

Sport	Try #1	Try #2	Try #3	Try #4	Try #5	Mean	Median	Mode	Range
Discuss									
Shot Put									
Javelin									
Curling									

Work Space:

Teacher: Photocopy one per student.

Name _____   Date _____

Directions: With your partner fill in your original curling distances. Fill in how/why you made improvements to your "stone" or surface using scientific principles. Repeat the curling game 5 times and record your new distances. Finally, make your conclusions.

Original Curling Distances					
New Curling Distances					

What changes did you make to your curling stone and/or playing surface and why?

_____
_____
_____
_____
_____

Conclusions:

_____
_____
_____
_____
_____

Teacher: Photocopy one per student.

Itsy Bitsy Book Report

Objective: SWBAT sequence and/or retell information

Grade Level: 3 - 6

Materials:
- Mini book sheets-attached (look at Pssst... section on how to construct)

Directions:
This page will save your day!!!! (We're not kidding!) Depending on which area of your curriculum you are studying, this blank book can be used to sequence events of a story, dates in history, steps of a scientific process, mathematical operations, stanzas in poetry, etc... The list honestly goes on and on. The booklet is numbered so that when it is folded, the responses will be in order. Here are some of our favorite ideas for using this book. Increase the level of difficulty according to your grade level/curriculum.

Page Number	Language Arts	Math	Social Studies	Science
1	Title of poem	Word Problem Title	The year	Lifecycle of a butterfly
2	Visualization of Stanza One	First... (Johnny had 5 apples.)	Event 1	Egg Stage
3	Visualization of Stanza Two	Next... (Johnny ate 3.)	Event 2	Pupa
4	Visualization of Stanza Three	Then...(Johnny picked 10 more apples from a tree.)	Event 3	Chrysalis
5	Visualization of Stanza Four	After That... (6 of Johnny's friends came by.)	Event 4	Butterfly
6	Visualization of Stanza Five	Suddenly... (They each took an equal amount of apples.)	Event 5	Picture of specific butterfly and 3 facts
7	New vocabulary and definitions	Question... (How many apples did Johnny have left?)	Culminating sentence of relevance of year	Picture of specific butterfly and 3 facts
8	How this poem made you feel	Answer... (Zero)	Personal opinion about that year	Picture of specific butterfly and 3 facts

2	1
3	8
4	7
5	6

Teacher: Photocopy one or more per student.

Pssst... Did You Hear The One About...?

In this section we are sharing with you some of our favorite all-purpose, no frills, fits-right-in-to-any-subject, definitions, games, and materials. They are a great asset when you are reviewing and/or practicing previously learned subject matter and skills. Trust us, these babies are truly lifesavers. Once you know them, they will be in your forever bag of tricks. The purpose here is to make your planning easier – especially when it's nine o'clock on a Sunday night and you just can't seem to plan anymore.

SWBAT = Students Will Be Able To

Clipboard Cruising

Using your class roster and a clipboard, cruise around the classroom taking notes on your students' progress.

Hot Dog and Hamburger Folds

These terms help students and adults visualize which way to fold a paper. To fold like a hot dog, fold paper vertically, just like a hot dog bun. To fold like a hamburger, fold paper horizontally, just like a hamburger bun.

Tic-Tac-Do You Know?

Divide class in half. Designate one team X and one team O. Draw a blank tic-tac-toe board on chalkboard/white board. Pose subject matter question/spelling word/math fact/comprehension question/vocabulary word & definition, etc... to one team. If answered correctly, their symbol is placed on the board. Repeat back and forth until one team successfully gets 3 symbols in a row. This game moves very quickly and can be played several times.

Give It a Shot!

This fast paced game will help your students review for every subject. Using flashcards and a chalkboard eraser, students will be able to score points for their team with every correct answer and/or basket made. Before you play, make a set of cards incorporating the skills you wish the class to review. (Examples: vocabulary words, math computation, and historical events...) To play, divide the class in half. Pick one student from Team A to read/solve the skill on the card. If the student answers correctly, Team A scores 2 points. The child is then allowed to take the eraser and "shoot" it into a basket for an additional score of 1 point. If the child is incorrect when answering the question, he/she is still able to "shoot" the eraser in hopes of getting that 1-point. Go back and forth between the teams until all cards are answered.

Flip Books

Use 3 pieces of paper to make your 6-page book. Place page 1 down. Place page 2 on top of page 1 leaving the bottom one inch of page one exposed. Place page 3 on top of page 2, leaving the bottom one inch of page 2 exposed. At this point you will have 3 staggered pages. Pick up stack and begin to fold top portion of pages backwards. You will begin to see that your original 3 steps meet the bottom 3 steps. Adjust your fold so that all steps are equal in size. Staple the top at the fold to bind book.

Mini Books

Hamburger fold an 8 ½ x 11 paper. Fold again like a hamburger. Once again, fold paper like a hamburger. Open paper up to its original form and then refold like a hamburger. Cut from center of fold down to the center point (where all lines intersect). Open paper again and then refold like a hotdog. Hold paper horizontally. Push ends toward center so it looks like a plus sign. Fold to form book.

Milk Jug Dice

Using 2 one-gallon milk jugs (empty and clean), you can make a super-sturdy and multi-purpose die. Cut off and discard the top portions of the two milk jugs just below the handles. You should now have 2 square shaped containers. Insert the open ends of containers into one another so you have one cube with six solid sides. Seal edges with clear tape to create a sturdier die.

Great Music!

Educational music that is also fun (and cool) for the older students is often hard to come by. The CD Here Comes Science by They Might Be Giants is simply FANTASTIC!!! From "meeting the elements" to speed and velocity, you will be amazed at how in depth the songs get. And a bonus... a DVD is included! If nothing else, stick it in your sub folder!

Untangled Circle

This is a wonderful activity to increase social skills and cooperation among class members. An even number of children will form a circle facing inward. Those standing opposite of each other will join their right hands. All left hands are randomly joined. Hands must not separate. Through a series of movements, the children must untangle themselves – always keeping their hands joined. They do not have to face the same direction when untangled. During the entire process, the students should be communicating with one another calmly and productively so that the group can work as a team to untangle themselves. They need to look at this like a chess game – thinking of the how one move will affect the next. They are finished when they are untangled and students are still holding hands in a circle.